The Red Coal

The Red Coal

POEMS BY

GERALD STERN

HOUGHTON MIFFLIN COMPANY BOSTON 1981

Library of Congress Cataloging in Publication Data
Stern, Gerald.
    The red coal.   I. Title.
    PS3569.T3888R37   811'.54   80–26050
    ISBN 0-395-30541-1
    ISBN 0-395-30542-X (pbk.)

Printed in the United States of America

P 10 9 8 7 6 5 4 3 2 1

My thanks to the editors of the following magazines and anthologies, in
which these poems previously appeared:
    The American Poetry Review: "Rotten Angel," "Modern Love,"
"Hanging Scroll," "The Shirt Poem," "The Angel Poem," "A Hundred
Years from Now," "The Poem of Liberation," "Your Animal." *Antaeus:*
"Pick and Poke," "Ice, Ice." *Field:* "There is Wind, There Are Matches,"
"Arthur's Lily." *Iowa Review:* "The War Against the Jews," "The Pi-
casso Poem," "For Night to Come." *Ironwood:* "One More Time the
Lambs." *Missouri Review:* "The Faces I Love," "The Sacred Spine," "In
These Shadows," "Days of 1978," "The Rose Warehouse." *The New
Yorker:* "Little White Sister," "The Roar." *Northwest Review:* "Dangerous
Cooks," "Good Friday, 1977," "Royal Manor Road," "Joseph Pockets,"
"No Wind." *Paris Review:* "Swan Song," "Immensity," "Elaine Com-
parone," "June First," "St. Patrick's Day, 1979," "The Red Coal," "Dear
Mole," "Here I Am Walking," "My Hand." *Pequod:* "Lord, Forgive a
Spirit," "Phipps Conservatory." *Poetry:* "Waving Good-by," "Potpourri,"
"I Remember Galileo," "Magritte Dancing," "Thinking About Shelley,"
"June Fourth," "Acacia," "Little Did the Junco Know." *Poetry East:*
"Cow Worship," "Visiting Florida Again," "These Birds." *Terra Poetica:*
"The-Way-We-Were Lounge."
    Pushcart V: "I Remember Galileo" (reprint). *Anthology of Magazine
Verse and Yearbook of American Poetry 1980:* "Modern Love" (reprint).
Anthology of Magazine Verse and Yearbook of American Poetry 1981:
"Your Animal" (reprint), "Days of 1978" (reprint).

I wish to express my gratitude to the John Simon Guggenheim Memorial
Foundation for the Fellowship which aided in the completion of this
book, and to the Commonwealth of Pennsylvania and the Pennsylvania
Council on the Arts for a Creative Writing Fellowship.

CONTENTS

The Red Coal

THE FACES I LOVE

Once and for all I will lie down here like a dead man,
letting the socialists walk over my face, letting the fascists
crawl through my veins, letting the Krishnas
poison me with their terrible saffron.

Once and for all I will lie here helpless and exhausted.
I will let dishonor rise from me like steam
and tears fall down on me like oily rain.

In the end my stillness will save me;
in the end the leopard will walk away from me in boredom
and trot after something living, something violent
and warm to excite him before his death.

In the end I will have my own chair.
I will pull the blinds down and watch my nose and mouth
in the blistered glass.
I will look back in amazement at what I did
and cry aloud for two more years, for four more years,
just to remember the faces, just to recall the names,
to put them back together —
the names I can't forget, the faces I love.

LITTLE WHITE SISTER

It was in Philadelphia that I first lived a life of deferment,
putting everything off until I could be at ease.
There, more than in New York and more than in Paris,
I lay for hours in bed, forgetting to eat, forgetting
to swim, dying of imperfection and loneliness.
It was in Vienna that I learned what it would be like
to live in two lives, and learned to wander between them;
and it was in the rotten underbelly
of western Pennsylvania that I was saved twice by a pear tree,
one time living and one time dead, and enslaved
once and for all by a patented iron grate
carrying words of terror through the yellow air.
    My ear betrayed me, my little white sister
glued to the side of my head, a shiny snail
twisted everywhere to catch the slightest
murmur of love, the smallest sobbing and breathing.
It wasn't the heart, stuck inside the chest
like a bloody bird, and it wasn't the brain,
dying itself from love; it was that messenger,
laughing as she whispered the soft words,
making kissing sounds with her red lips,
moaning with pleasure for the last indignity.

SWAN SONG

A bunch of old snakeheads down by the pond
carrying on the swan tradition — hissing
inside their white bodies, raising and lowering their heads
like ostriches, regretting only the sad ritual
that forced them to waddle back into the water
after their life under the rocks, wishing they could slither again
as they did in the old days, wishing they could lie again in the sun
and dream of spreading their terrifying wings;
wishing, this time, they could sail through the sky like horses,
their tails rigid, their white manes fluttering,
their mouths open, their sharp teeth flashing,
drops of mercy pouring from their eyes,
bolts of wisdom from their foreheads.

IMMENSITY

Nothing is too small for my sarcasm. I know
a tiny moth that crawls over the rug
like an English spy sneaking through the Blue Forest,
and I know a Frenchman that hangs on the closet door
singing *chanson* after *chanson* with his smashed thighs.
I will examine my life through curled threads
and short straws and little drops of food.
I will crawl around with my tongue out, growing
more and more used to the dirty webs hanging
between the ridges of my radiator and the huge
smudges in that distant sky up there, beginning
more and more to take on the shape of some great design.
   This is the way to achieve immensity, and this is the
only way to get ready for death, no matter what Immanuel Kant
and the English philosophers say about the mind,
no matter what the gnostics say, crawling
through their vile blue, sneezing madly in the midst of that
life of theirs, weighed down by madness and sorrow.

ROTTEN ANGEL

My friends, still of this world, follow me to the bottom of the river
tripping over roots and cutting themselves on the dry grass.
They are all over on the left side, drinking beer and crying,
and I am there by myself waiting for the rotten angel.
For my sake it hasn't rained for twenty days
and all the old jetties are showing up again in the water.
I can reach my arms up into the second row of branches
and pull down clumps of dead leaves and barrel hoops.
I finally find my clearing and fall down in the dirt,
exhausted from thirty minutes of fighting for air.
I put an x on the ground and start marking off
a place for the gravel, the rhododendron and the iron bird.
My friends stand above me, a little bored by my death
and a little tired of the flies and the sad ritual.
— How I would love it if I could really be buried here,
a mile away from my house in this soft soil.
I think the state could do this for me — they could give me
a few feet of earth — they could make an exception.
I tell you it really matters and all that talk
about so many cents' worth of fat and so many grams
of water is really just fake humility.
I would hate being dusted on the ocean or put in a drawer
for perpetuity — I want to be connected
with life as long as possible, I want to disappear slowly,

as gruesome as that sounds, so there is time
for those who want to see me in my own light
and get an idea of how I made my connections
and what I looked at and dreamed about
and what the river smelled like from this island
and how the grackles sounded when they landed
in the polished trees and how the trucks sounded
charging up 611 carrying the culture
of Philadelphia into the mountains
and how the angel must have gasped as he swam
back to the shore and how he must have dipped
his head in the green water to escape the gnats
swarming after him in the dirty sunlight
a million miles from his New York and his Baltimore and his Boston.

DANGEROUS COOKS

I am serving my own head on a platter, as Ensor did.
I am a plucked chicken hanging in the air.
I am lying on the floor with a pig's body and a pince-nez.
I am dropping tears in a frying pan.
  Always I am in the middle of everything.
My voice is in the woods;
my hands are in the water;
my face is in the clouds, like a hot sun.

GOOD FRIDAY, 1977

Suddenly there are hundreds of fishermen on the road,
wearing hats and waders and thick shirts and badges.
Their cars and trucks are lined up on the lawns and ditches.
Dozens are in the water already,
side by side, casting and reeling in the foam,
ending Christianity once and for all on this small river.

PICK AND POKE

I began this fall by watching a thin red squirrel
sneak out of my neighbor's wrecked Simca and run over
a pile of bricks into one of its small forests.
Then and there I set up my watch
so I could follow that sweet redness
in and out of our civilization.
    It would have been so easy with the old English taxi
at Pick and Poke. It stands six feet high,
like a small coach waiting for its shabby prince
to walk through his porch posts and his barrels
and mount the leather seat in two short steps,
whereas the Simca is practically buried in the leaves,
its glass is gone, and half its insides are rotted.
But it isn't size, and it isn't even location;
it has something to do with character, and something
to do with ideas, and something, even, to do
with the secret history of France, and of England.
After two weeks I saw everything
as clearly as a squirrel does — a Simca
is part of nature, lying halfway between
the wet maples and the field of tarpaulin,
the armrest is a perch, the back seat is a warehouse,
and the gearshift is a small dangerous limb.
But my loyalty is mostly to England,

so I found myself wandering down
day after day to the big yard at Pick and Poke.
There I studied the square wheelbarrow
and the lawn furniture — I walked around the taxi,
measuring the giant wheels and fancy tool box,
and I sat in the back and rapped on the glass partition
over the jump seats, ordering my driver to carry me
down the river to New Hope and Philadelphia.
After just a few hours I understood the English spirit,
and after a day I even understood the English garden
from watching the scattered shutters and old storm windows.
    We here in France salute the English.
We admire them for their tolerance and shyness.
We love them for their geography and their music,
their hatred of theory and their bad food,
their optimism and love of animals.
We in America are more like red squirrels: we live
from roof to roof, our minds are fixed on the great
store of the future, our bodies are worn out from leaping;
we are weary of each other's faces, each other's dreams.
We sigh for some understanding, some surcease,
some permanence, as we move from tree to tree,
from wire to wire, from empty hole to empty hole,
singing, singing, always singing, of that amorous summer.

ROYAL MANOR ROAD

It would be worth it to go ninety miles out of your way
to see these cows eat and sleep and nuzzle in the mud.
It would be worth it to leave the tables at Grand Ticino
and walk down Thompson Street talking about the eyes —
"Are they the eyes of Kora, are they soft and slanted;
are they the eyes of Juno and drunken Hathor?"
All my reading, all my difficult reading
would be worth it as I stood in the weeds
watching them run up like kittens, watching them
crowd each other for little tastes of clover and hepatica.
To reach my hand inside
and touch the bony forehead and the stiff hair
would be worth it.

MODERN LOVE

In a month all these frozen waterfalls
will be replaced by Dutchman's breeches
and I will drive down the road
trying to remember what it was like
in late February and early March.
It will be 72 degrees on March 24th
and I will see my first robin
on the roof of the Indian Rock Inn.
My wife and I will go in to stare at the chandelier
and eat, like starved birds, in front of the fireplace.
I know now that what I'll do
all through supper is plan my walk
from Bristol, Pa., to the canal museum.
I will exhaust her with questions about old hotels
and how much water I should carry
and what shoes I should wear,
and she will meet me with sweetness and logic
before we break up over money and grammar and lost love.
Later the full moon will shine through our windshield
as we zigzag up the river
dragging our tired brains, and our hearts, after us.
I will go to bed thinking of George Meredith
lying beside a red sword
and I will try to remember how his brain smoked

as he talked to his wife in her sleep and twisted her words.
— Where I will go in the six hours before I wake up freezing
I don't know, but I do know
I will finally lie there with my twelve organs in place,
wishing I were in a tea palace, wishing
I were in a museum in France, wishing
I were in a Moorish movie house in Los Angeles.
I will walk downstairs singing because it is March 25th
and I will walk outside to drink my coffee on the stone wall.
There will still be drops of snow on the side of the hill
as we plant our peas and sweep away the birdseed.
Watch me dig and you will see me
dream about justice, and you will see me
dream about small animals, and you will see me
dream about warm strawberries.
From time to time I will look over
and watch her dragging sticks and broken branches
across the road. We are getting ready
for summer. We are working in the cold
getting ready. Only thirty more days and the moon
will shine on us again as we drive to Hellertown
to see Jane Fonda grimace, and drive back
after midnight through the white fields,
looking for foxes in the stubble,
looking for their wild eyes, burning with fear and shyness,
in the stunted remains of last summer's silk forest.

THE WAR AGAINST THE JEWS

Look how peaceful these wooden figures are, going to their death.
How happy they were to go instead of me.
They love to march back and forth under the iron clock.
One tips his hat endlessly to a mother and her three children.
One dries his tears in front of the water fountain.
They bump their heads as they bend down to drink.

Over there a German soldier is blowing his whistle.
He was carved while he still could remember his mother's garden.
How glad he was to go to Poland.
How young he felt in his first pair of boots.

I would give anything to bring them back:
to let them sit again on the polished benches;
to let them see the great glass roof again;
to rush through the noisy crowd screaming
"Stop! It's a dream! It's a dream!
Go back to your shuls. Go back to your mother's garden.
O wooden figures, go back, go back."

LITTLE DID THE JUNCO KNOW

Little did the junco know who he was keeping company with this
    Christmas,
he and the nuthatch and the chickadee and the red sparrow,
racing back and forth between the bag of fat
and the pan of birdseed under the dead vine.

Little did those sweethearts know who was in their midst,
with his round eye and his small head and his plump body
rolling after the neck like a mop keeping up with its tiny handle.

And little did he know himself why people fought over him
and waved him in the air and sent him out
morning after morning in the first light —
that soft gray one with the long tail
and the monotonous voice,
gorging himself at the battered aluminum pan.

LORD, FORGIVE A SPIRIT

So what shall we do about this angel,
growing dizzy every time he climbs a ladder,
crying over his old poems.
I walk out into the garden and there he is,
watering the lilies and studying the digitalis.
He is talking to his own invisible heart;
he is leaking blood.
   The sun shines on him all day long
as he wanders from bush to bush.
His eyes flash with fire, his eyelashes blaze and
his skin shines like brass,
but he trips in the dirt just like any gardener, or grieving poet.
   I watch him walk beside the cactus;
I watch him kneel in front of the wet horsetails;
I touch his lips.
I write all day. I sit beside him all
day long and write the garbled words.
I sit in the sun and fill a whole new book
with scrawls and symbols.
I watch the sky as he talks about the gold leaf
and the half-forgotten ruins; I watch the words
drift from his mouth like clouds.
I watch the colors change from orange to red
to pink as he tries to remember his old words —

his old songs, his first human songs —
lost somewhere in the broken glass and the cinders,
a foot below the soft nails and the hinges.

ELAINE COMPARONE

I love to sit down
in front of my lilac fence
and watch the wind blow through the pointed leaves.

If I could do exactly what I wanted
I would move a harpsichord into my back yard
and ask Elaine Comparone to play for me all morning.

My friend Barbara Dazzle said she would move
her dining-room furniture out and put the long red box
in the middle of the gardenias and the hanging ivy.

Either way I would listen to the steel bird sing
and watch Elaine shift back and forth on her chair,
torn between my love of Domenico Scarlatti
and my desire to lay my head down on her flowery lap.

My joy begins as I dream of a woman blushing
beside her stone wall, and my pain begins
when she turns into a shadow, with notes falling
around her like blossoms on the wet grass.

I run through the garden shouting kiss me, kiss me!
In one more day the petals will be curled and brown,

they will lie piled up like dead leaves —
smeared on the walk like blood;

oh in one hour the great tree will stand there shaking
and the box will be carried out like a heavy coffin
and Elaine Comparone will sit with her hands in her lap,
in the cold air, rushing back to the city,
remembering the notes falling on the ground
and the red spikes inside the creamy blossoms
and the new leaves making their way like tiny crescendos
in the drawing rooms of Petrograd and Stockholm,
dreaming of sunlight and rain and endless dancing.

ICE, ICE

When I woke up this morning I knew there was horror, I
remembered the rain last night and I knew the ice had
come. I knew the doves would be dragging their stiff tails and
I knew the yard would be filled with broken branches. I sing
this for Hubert Humphrey, dead last night, and I sing it
for the silent birds, and I sing it
for the frozen trees and the bouquet of frozen buds,
and the tiny puffs of smoke now rising from our chimneys
like the smoke of cave men rising from their fissures,
their faces red with wisdom, their dirty hands scraping
grease from the stones and shaking ashes from their beds,
their black eyes weeping over the chunks of fire,
their tears turning to ice as they leave the circle.

ONE MORE TIME THE LAMBS

One more time the hard green daffodils are growing
in clumps beside the stone wall and the cesspool.
They go with the melancholy and the cold rain,
with the black trees and the frozen seedpods.
I resist every effort at exhaustion
and walk by all the traps as if nothing were happening.
I am going to go through it with ease,
no bitterness and no indecision this time.
Again the river rises and again the logs
and oil drums float by;
again we are sleeping, again we wait
for the sun to make our lives more pleasant.
One more time the lamb rests his soft head
on the stone culvert, one more time he lies there
cool and thoughtful, one more time he drops his red blood
on the dirty ice. I study the thin green trees
and the blue water hanging in the air;
I stay awake for two long days and start my
sleep at four in the evening. The wind is my love,
the rain is my love, the torn lamb is my love.
The sun goes off and on like a white eye
watching. I wake up singing,
floating, bursting, inside my sweet shelter.

THE SACRED SPINE

It will always be invisible, it will
have hair on it, but that will be false,
and skin, but that will be stretched over
the branches like a sweater dipped in alum.
It will hang from the mouth
like a piece of paper or a large caterpillar.
It will twist over doubly
like a ravenous birch.
It will lie rigid.
It will scream out,
trying to find a position.
It will turn in pain,
trying to escape, trying to release
itself, trying to live again
without fear and exhaustion,
trying to float once more, trying to rest, trying to rise
in the fine dust and the feathers,
in the wet leaves and the grass and the flowers,
on the bleached wood and the pillows and the warm air
and the weeds and the water.

I REMEMBER GALILEO

I remember Galileo describing the mind
as a piece of paper blown around by the wind,
and I loved the sight of it sticking to a tree
or jumping into the back seat of a car,
and for years I watched paper leap through my cities;
but yesterday I saw the mind was a squirrel caught crossing
Route 80 between the wheels of a giant truck,
dancing back and forth like a thin leaf,
or a frightened string, for only two seconds living
on the white concrete before he got away,
his life shortened by all that terror, his head
jerking, his yellow teeth ground down to dust.

It was the speed of the squirrel and his lowness to the ground,
his great purpose and the alertness of his dancing,
that showed me the difference between him and paper.
Paper will do in theory, when there is time
to sit back in a metal chair and study shadows;
but for this life I need a squirrel,
his clawed feet spread, his whole soul quivering,
the hot wind rushing through his hair,
the loud noise shaking him from head to tail.
    O philosophical mind, O mind of paper, I need a squirrel
finishing his wild dash across the highway,
rushing up his green ungoverned hillside.

POTPOURRI

I see my wife struggling in the dirt
with her roses and her iris and I watch her
domesticate every mountain within ten miles,
but I know it is the delicate spring things,
the bloodroot and the columbine, that move her.
I think of the great space between her and
the wild domestic poets I hear reading at the Moat
and the Lavender Gate and I understand
exactly the difference between them;
and when I watch her on the flowered sheets,
with her eyes finally closed
and her purple T-shirt already wet with sleep,
I understand a delicacy and a mournfulness
that neither Nietzsche my one love
nor Van Gogh my other
could help me with, for all their knowledge and purity.
    Tonight a huge black rose
sits on the oak chest
beside the silver candlesticks,
dominating the small room with
its size and odor.
I am sitting down eating strawberries
and turning the rose on its thick stem.
Across the room a potpourri waits,

like a rich grave full of herbs and spices,
for the moist petals;
and under the light a bouquet of wild daisies
with three round thistles on the outer edges
is half buried inside a tin pitcher.
— What I will do after a minute is walk outside
to pluck the strings
and I will feel pleasure in the darkness
that will unite me forever with the sleepless Italians
and the waterless Greeks beside their stone jars.
In the morning we will sit on the metal chairs
and drink coffee and exchange dreams;
tonight I will sit there alone, listening to trucks
go up the highway and getting small glimpses
of the sky between the eaves and the black maples.
I will do two things before I go upstairs:
I will see if the thorn tree is still living
and I will put a blue trumpet in my shirt pocket.
On my way in I will practice a little
breathing, a little emptiness,
and I will listen to the crazy night bird
with my hand against the pillar and my head bowed
so I can lie down in wisdom and luxury.

MAGRITTE DANCING

Every night I have to go to bed twice,
once by myself, suddenly tired and angry,
and once when my wife turns the weak light on
and stumbles over my shoes into the bathroom.
Some nights there is a third time — the phone
is ringing and I rush out into the hall;
my heart is pounding but nobody is there
and I have to go back to bed empty-handed
just as my brain was beginning to pick up signals.
This time it takes me all night to get back to sleep.
I don't sink again into the heavy pillow
but lie there breathing, trying to push
everything back into its own channel.
For hours I watch the dark and then gradually
I begin watching the light; by that time
I am thinking again about snow tires and I am thinking
about downtown Pittsburgh and I am thinking
about the turtles swimming inside their brown willows.
I look at the morning with relief, with something close
to pleasure that I still have one more day,
and I dance the dance of brotherliness and courtliness
as first my neighbor the postman, pocked and pitted,
goes crawling off in his early morning bitterness
and then my neighbor the body man goes bouncing away,

his own car rusty and chromeless, his T-shirt torn,
his eyes already happy from his first soothing beer.
— The dance I dance is to the tune of Magritte
banging his bedposts on a square mountain,
and Oskar Schlemmer floating up a stairway,
and Pablo Picasso looking inside a woman's head.
I dance on the road and on the river and
in the wet garden, all the time living in Crete
and pre-war Poland and outer Zimbabwe,
as through my fingers and my sparkling hair
the morning passes, first the three loud calls
of the bluejay, then the white door slamming,
then the voices rising and falling in sudden harmony.

THE SHIRT POEM

It is ten years since I have seen these shirts
screaming from their hangers, crying for blood and money.
They shake their empty arms
and grow stiff as they wait for the light to come.
I open the door an inch at a time to let them out
and start candles all over the room to soothe them.
— Gone is sweetness in that closet, gone is the dream
of brotherhood, the affectionate meeting
of thinkers and workers inside a rented hall.
Gone are the folding chairs, gone forever
the sacred locking of elbows under the two flags.

On Sunday night they used to sing for hours
before the speeches. Once the rabbis joined them
and religion and economics were finally combined in exile.
"Death is a defect," they sang, and threw their hats
on the floor. "We will save nature from death,"
they shouted, and ended up dancing on the small stage,
the dark crows and the speckled doves finally arm in arm.

They will never come back — in a thousand years;
it is not like bringing a forest back, putting a truckload
of nitrogen in the soil, burning some brush,
planting seedlings, measuring distance —

these are people, whose secret habits we no longer know,
how they tore their bread and what designs they made on the tablecloth,
what they thought about as they stared through the warped glass,
what the melting ice meant to them.

Poor dead ones! Forgive me for the peace I feel as I walk out
to the mailbox. Forgive me for the rich life I lead.
Forgive me for the enormous budget and the bureaucracy and the
        permanent army.
When I come home from New York City I stand outside
for twenty minutes and look out at the lights.
Upstairs the shirts are howling and snapping,
marching back and forth in front of the silver radiator.
In a minute I will be up there closing doors
and turning on lamps.
I will take the papers out of my coat pocket
and put them in their slots.
I will think of you with your own papers and your rubber bands.
What is my life if not a substitute for yours,
and my dream a substitute for your dream?
Lord, how it has changed, how we have
made ourselves strange, how embarrassing the words
sound to us, how clumsy and half-hearted we are.

I want to write it down before it's forgotten,
how we lived, what we believed in;
most of all to remember the giants
and how they walked, always with white hair,
always with long white hair hanging down over their collars,
always with red faces, always bowing and listening,
their heads floating as they moved through the small crowd.

Outside the wind is blowing
and the snow is piling up against the pillars.
I could go back in a minute to the synagogue in Beechview
or the Carnegie Library on the North Side.

I could turn and shake hands with the tiny man
sitting beside me and wish him peace.
I could stand in front and watch the stained-glass
window rattle in its frame and the guest speaker
climb into the back seat of his car.

I am writing about the past because there was
still affection left then, and other sorrows;
because I believed my white silk scarf could save me,
and my all-day walks;
because when I opened my window the smell
of snow made me tremble with pleasure;
because I was a head taller than the tiny man sitting next to me;
because I was always the youngest;
because I believed in Shelley;
because I carried my entire memory along with me in the summer;
because I stared at the old men with loving eyes;
because I studied their fallen shoulders and their huge hands;
because I found relief only in my drawings;
because I knew the color and texture of every rug and every chair
and every lampshade in my first house.

Give this to Rabbi Kook who always arrived
with his clothes on fire and stood between the mourners,
singing songs against death in all three languages
at the crowded wall, in the dark sunlight.

And give this to Malatesta who believed in
the perfect world and lived in it as he moved
from country to country, for sixty years, tasting the
bread, tasting the meat, always working,
cursing the Church, cursing the State,
seeing through everything, always seeing the heart
and what it wanted, the beautiful cramped heart.

My shirts are fine. They dance
by themselves along the river
and bleed a little as they fall down on the dirty glass.

If they had knees they would try to
crawl back up the hill and stop the trucks
or march back and forth singing their swamp songs.
They see me coming and fly up to the roof;
they are like prehistoric birds,
half leaping, half sailing by.
They scream with cold, they break through the hall window
and knock over baskets and push open doors
until they stand there in place, in back of the neckties,
beside the cold plaster, in the dust
above the abandoned shoes, weeping in silence,
moaning in exhaustion,
getting ready again to live in darkness.

JUNE FIRST

Some blossoms are so white and luscious, when they
hold their long thin hands up you strip them for love
and scatter them on the ground as you walk;

and some birds look at you as if there were no
great line drawn between their lives and yours,
as if you drank together from the same cement;

and some pods spin in the wind as if you would not pick
them up gingerly to see if they had wings
and then would not break them open to see what made them
fall, to study their visceras.

I touch you as I would the sawdust in the eaves
or the crazy buttercups in the middle of the mulepath
or the frightening foil
jumping and leaping in front of the oily grackles;

and I touch you as I touch the grass, my body falls down on the ground
and I pull at the roots as I watch you in the limbs
bending down to avoid the red blossoms,
hiding in the leaves,

reaching up like the tallest dryad,
your curved arms and your jeweled fingers
waving slowly again in the hot sun.

THINKING ABOUT SHELLEY

Arm over arm I swam out into the rain,
across from the cedars and the rickety conveyor.
I had the quarry all to myself again,
even the path down to the muddy bank.
Every poet in the world was dead but me.
Yeats was dead, Victor Hugo was dead,
Cavafy was dead — with every kick I shot
a jet of water into the air — you could see
me coming a mile away, my shoulders rolling
the way my father's did. I started moving
out into the open between the two islands,
thinking about Shelley and his milky body.
No one had been here before — I was the first
poet to swim in this water — I would be the
mystery, I would be the source
for all the others to come. The rivers of China
were full of poets, the lakes of Finland, the ponds
of southern France, but no one in Pennsylvania
had swum like this across an empty quarry.
I remember at the end I turned on my back
to give my neck a rest; I remember floating
into the weeds and letting my shoulders touch
the greasy stones; I remember lying
on the coarse sand reaching up for air.

This happened in June before the berries were out,
before the loosestrife covered the hills, before
the local sinners took off their clothes and waded
like huge birds in the cold water.
It was the first warm day and I was
laboring in this small sea.
I remember how I hoped my luck would last;
I remember the terror of the middle
and how I suddenly relaxed after passing the islands;
I remember it was because of Shelley
that I changed my innocent swim
into such a struggle,
that it was because of Shelley
I dragged my body up, tired and alive,
to the small landing under the flowering highway,
full of silence now and clarity.

COW WORSHIP

I love the cows best when they are a few feet away
from my dining-room window and my pine floor,
when they reach in to kiss me with their wet
mouths and their white noses.
I love them when they walk over the garbage cans
and across the cellar doors,
over the sidewalk and through the metal chairs
and the birdseed.
— Let me reach out through the thin curtains
and feel the warm air of May.
It is the temperature of the whole galaxy,
all the bright clouds and clusters,
beasts and heroes,
glittering singers and isolated thinkers
at pasture.

JOSEPH POCKETS

Have you ever lived through seven fat years and grown soft
from eating lamb and bulgur? I remember lawyers
standing in line for doughnuts and geniuses painting
the walls of Idlewild Airport. Two things happened
to make me remember: one was a film about the 30's,
put together to show the times as primitive
in the Eisenstein style; the other was my invasion
of Kaufmann's department store to buy a suit
from the crowd of salesmen dressed up in plaids and stripes,
to go with my new dignity and ferocity.

In *The Hunger March* thousands of lean men converge
on Washington in sheepskin coats and fedoras.
Already the cap was dead; already the workingmen
had started to move out of their small houses.
The joy was watching them go through city after city.
The joy was watching the camera catch their happiness
as they half ran down the old highways,
singing of empty stomachs and freezing rain.

In *The Ford Massacre* the figures move
in a rush across the screen; they either are buried
down the tracks in puffs of smoke or stand
on top of you, screaming for justice in silent voices.

The seven lean years came first — they lasted seven years;
the seven fat years lasted over twenty-five.
Joseph comes later. He turns the past into a dream
and shows us how we lived and what disappeared
as we left the 40's and went into the 50's.
I'm back in Pittsburgh now; it's only here
and maybe Detroit and maybe a little Chicago
that there are Joseph pockets where you can see
the dream turned around and the darkness illuminated,
some of the joy explained, some of the madness —
Chicago, St. Louis, Minneapolis, Boston, Buffalo.

When I walked into the lobby I felt like a visitor.
I sat beside a black-haired woman with a shawl
who knew what I was radiating and touched me
on the little wooden arm. I lived in a Joseph
pocket there and when I left she touched me
again as if to say, "Well, wait for me. The marches
will be over in fifteen minutes and we can walk
through Father Demo Square past our brick mansion
where we could imagine living in half-dark rooms,
drinking tea from flowered cups and sleeping
in modern anarchy under the blue skylight."

When I walked into Kaufmann's I carried the past
with me like a colored stone in my pocket.
Two diplomats walked over, their eyes showing
almost no pity, their voices cold and resentful
as they abandoned me in front of the hooded sweaters.
I had to look at suits myself; I had to learn
about European cuts and what vents did for my body
and what my sloping shoulders needed and where the
sleeves should end and where the collar should be,
without a sucking salesman hanging on
and dragging me around from rack to rack.

I will be living in Pittsburgh one more month.
All the time I am here I will move between
my hatred of Frick and my love of the forty bridges.
Over and over again I will walk downtown
through Market Square and past the Oyster House,
or I will drive through South Side and Mt. Washington
wishing the Japanese could see these hills.
This is the city where art was brought in by the trainload
and Mellon money is wasted to bring Grace Kelly
on stage to read poems about birds and their transcendence.
This is the city where Iron is our drink, we say, "Iron,"
we say, "Give me Iron," we say, "Piss on watery Miller's."
This is the city where I lay down like a twisted
poppy to read my Marlowe and my Pound.

I can look down the river from my back room.
It's worth a million dollars. I can see
the lights hanging from broomsticks and the cars
bouncing up and down on the crooked boulevard.
But the best view is ten o'clock in the morning;
the sun is behind me then and I can see
the light shining down on the whole city.
I want to float on that river — what dark legs
will push me, what silk hand will carry me
across the plain to the first row of mountains,
or drop me, singing, into the other river
beside a coal barge or a sleek cruiser?

My sister is buried in Carrick in the Jewish cemetery
three miles from the Liberty Tubes, beside my grandmother,
Libby Barach, and my grandfather, B. Barach,
both of them resting above her like two old friends.
For once I feel cut off and except for the presence
of the blue Nova in front of the service building
I might be in a Jewish graveyard in Poland,
crowded with souls, everyone a stranger.

I borrow a book from the bleak office and open
to the page to be read at the graveside of a sister.
I ask her first to remember her shocking death
and all the clumsiness and sadness of her leaving.
I ask her to describe — as she remembers it —
how I stood in front of her white coffin
and stared at the mourners in our small living room.
I ask her to think again about the two peach trees,
how close together they were, how tiny their fruit was,
forty years ago in the light rain,
wherever she is, whatever sweet wing she's under.

This is my last Joseph pocket. I am going
back to New York City. O Japanese,
you will love this place; you will spend a week
visiting junk stores and eating steaks and buying
boots and dishes to take with you back to Asia.
What I'll do is talk to the glass buildings
and explain myself. I think I'll stand in one place
to say good-by. I think I'll leave in the snow
with the wind blowing down the alley and the cars
going ten miles an hour up the Parkway, the cinder trucks
moving along in convoys, big clouds of steam
rising up from the river, all the sorrows
of life disappearing like drops of snow
as we pick up speed going east on the empty turnpike.

PHIPPS CONSERVATORY

Pittsburgh, 1978

Whoever wants to can live a lifetime in this herb garden,
rubbing leaves and sighing,
making choices among the mints and the scented geraniums.
He can listen to the flute and watch the girls
come one at a time into the arms of the shrill satyr.
He can walk through the borders and bend down like a stiff king
over the yellow marigolds.
He can sit on the lover's plank
and wail with joy
in his newfound misery
or talk to the Pole walking lightly and sweetly away
with seeds in his pocket, wrapped in tissue paper,
ready to burst with life on his rich hillside.

DAYS OF 1978

This is the only thing that clarifies my life,
this beautiful old living room
with the pink walls and the mohair sofa.
I walk out every night singing
a little song from Gus Williams or W. C. Handy.
I throw my yellow scarf around my neck
and pull my cap down over my eyes.
Even here I am dressed up,
walking through the light flakes and the ice puddles.
— Tonight I will think about Cavafy
and the way he wept on his satin pillow,
remembering the days of 1903.
I will compare my life to his:
the sorrows of Alexandria,
the lights on the river;
the dead kings returning to Syria,
the soap in my bath.
— Later I will lie on my own pillow
with the window open and the blinds up,
weeping a little myself at the thick blankets
and the smoking candles
and the stack of books,
a new sweetness and clarity beginning
to monopolize my own memory.

NO WIND

Today I am sitting outside the Dutch Castle
on Route 30 near Bird in Hand and Blue Ball,
watching the Amish snap their suspenders at the sunglasses.
I am dreaming of my black suit again
and the store in Paradise where I will be fitted out for life.
   A small girl and I recognize each other
from our former life together in Córdoba.
We weep over the plastic tote bags, the apple combs and the laughing
      harmonicas,
and fall down on the hot carpet
remembering the marble forest
of the Great Mosque
and the milky walls
of the Jewish quarter.
   I will see her again in 800 years
when all this is sorted out.
I give it that much time,
based on the slack mind,
the dirty drinking water and the slow decay.
I give it at least that much time
before we lie down again in the tiny lilacs
and paper love houses of the next age.

JUNE FOURTH

Today as I ride down Twenty-fifth Street I smell honeysuckle
rising from Shell and Victor Balata and K-Diner.
The goddess of sweet memory is there
staggering over fruit and drinking old blossoms.
A man in white socks and a blue T-shirt
is sitting on the grass outside Bethlehem Steel
eating lunch and dreaming.
Before he walks back inside he will be changed.
He will remember when he stands again under the dirty windows
a moment of great misgiving and puzzlement
just before sweetness ruined him and thinking
tore him apart. He will remember lying
on his left elbow studying the sky,
and the loss he felt, and the sudden freedom,
the mixture of pain and pleasure — terror and hope —
what he calls "honeysuckle."

THE ANGEL POEM

My broken wing is on the left near the large joint
that separates me so crazily from half the others.
I think of trees and how they break apart
in the wind, how sometimes a huge branch
will hang in strips, what would be skin
in humans or angels, and how the flesh
is like pulp, and almost blood-red where the break is.

I tend to drag the wing because the pain
in lifting it is too much for me to stand.
That part of me that is still human recalls
what pain in the shoulder can be, and I remember
not only the sharp stabs when I had to turn
but the stiffness that made me keep my arm at my side
and forced me to plan my eating and my sad sleeping.

As far as birds, I am more like a pigeon than a hawk.
I think I am one of those snow-white pigeons with gold
eyes and a candy-corn beak, with a ruffled
neck — a huge white hood — and ruffled
legs, like flowers or long white pantaloons,
shamelessly exposed under my white dress
and hopelessly drooping when I run in
fear and slip and fall on the dirty newspapers.

I fly with shame, when I fly, but mostly I sit
quietly or rise with effort to do my dance,
my head moving back and forth like a loose pendulum.

My main thought is how I can translate pain
into a form that I can understand,
so I break a wing or bruise my foot; but the wound
is more like panic, more like flying
without a shadow or flying in darkness,
something like the human dream when fear
makes them rise out of a sound sleep
and move without control above their bodies,
along the ceiling or through the closed windows,
pushing and yelling as they fall through the glass.
Either way we both have bloody feathers and
wake up groggy, sitting on the foot of the bed
listening to the birds slow down and the day start,
thinking about the dream and its double meaning.

I have looked myself up in the Jefferson Market Library,
in the pink basement where the ghosts of hundreds
of coiners and draft dodgers are still standing
under the arches, waiting to be dragged away.
Sometimes I sit there for hours reading about winged
servants and the mountains of justice and
the hierarchies of the Moors and the Akkadians.
I know — if anything — I am one of the million
Enoch encountered on his first trip to Heaven.
I sit against a freezing wall — my place is
forever against a freezing wall — my hands
hanging loosely down from my knees, a black cat
of Heaven rubbing up against my leg.
I know I am also the dark part of the leaf,
that I walk upright, that I am half snow, half fire,
that I can move like light from one end of the house to the other,
that I have something in common with Tammuz, and with Shelley.

I am wearing my long gray coat so I can hide
whatever I have to inside like stiff parchment.
I walk upstairs to look at the stained-glass windows
and touch the yellow stars and ruby petals
or move along the shelves, reaching at random
for the literature that will change my life.
I love this library above all others — I love
the two stone heads and the huge painted doors,
and I love standing outside underneath the pillars
and the great carved seal of New York City,
with all that Bavarian madness above me,
the clock and the chimneys and the turrets and the gargoyles,
a step away from the drowned lion on
one side and the fenced-in Greening on the other.
I wait for fifteen minutes, helping couples
move their heavy strollers, telling time
to Temple blonds dragging their sacred books,
and talking sweetly to Vichians and Spinozists.
Across the street is Balducci's where lamb chops go
for thirty dollars a pound and salmon is guarded
by Cuban soldiers; and just up Sixth is the flower
store, loaded with carnations and chrysanthemums,
where I was taken for a city inspector
with my yellow tablet and my blue jacket.

I start my walk at seven o'clock. Maybe
I'll reach the Port Authority by eight-thirty or nine.
All those who live in pain go on fixed walks
between two stations and mark the passage with drops
of blood. They push against each other, bruising
their delicate shoulders and legs — who would know
that one man's stomach is gone, that one has ankles
the size of balloons, that one is in terror
of impotence, that one has blood in her throat.
Dreiser is there pitying the dying poor,
Dostoevsky is studying the black sky,

Balzac is making new souls out of the dust.
They wear wings over their leather coats
and walk through mud as I walk over cement
and shout at the horses blocking their narrow paths.
When I reach Fourteenth I am practically running — past
the Greenwich Savings Bank and Corby's Bar,
past the dead pigeon and the Vitamin Quota.
I start to sing at Eighteenth Street across
from Wanamaker's lost department store — a kind
of Parthenon in the heart of the old soft goods —
and make my turn at Twenty-third past the empty
Paradise Cafeteria. I stop, lovingly
and longingly, in the lobby of the Chelsea
to look at the marble and dream about my life
as a man of letters, coming down the elevator
and standing outside in front of the bronze plaques
before I go to the nearest Blarney Stone
to eat my stew and think about my future.

On Eighth Avenue I am joined by the others
and we make our way down our own Dolorosa
like chirping grasshoppers and gurgling pigeons.
At ten to eight we walk into the empty lobby
of the New Yorker to look at the Moonie squads
and stop our music as we enter the corridor —
the six blocks between Thirty-fourth and Fortieth —
filled with every charm from disco centers
to cheap clothes to Spanish groceries;
adult book stores and movies and topless dancers;
readers and advisers; pimps and baby whores.
We set up headquarters beside the Trailways
in competition with the Children of Love,
but music is illegal at the Port Authority
so we put down our combs and potatoes
and walk away — like the others — with crushed vision.
— I have one hope, that we can leave together

by one of the upper gates and come slowly
into Sea Isle City or Asbury Park,
piping our souls away, singing all day
with no constraints — no bus drivers, no policemen,
no music teachers or critics or wise widows —
in French and Italian, Greek if we want to, or Slovak,
hymns and love songs, ballads and madrigals,
rattling the windows and shaking the sweet highways.

I think the sea and the sea air will mend
my stiff arm; I know that I will float
for hours in the icy water, humming
my new poems; I know that when the others
go, like mist, or gray jelly, or tiny crabs,
I will lie on the sand and make my own imprint,
seven or eight feet this time, a giant
sand angel, with footprints like a bear's,
with delicate hair, oh delicate hair on the brown
hill, and deep holes where my elbows are,
and little shivery markings where I turned
and moved my arms up and down through the soft valleys.

I will stay only long enough to watch one child — or two —
discover the image and run up to the iron benches
shouting, "An angel, an angel, there was an angel lying
on our beach; he was ten feet tall and his wings
were curved at the top like the white bird at school.
We saw him fly over the old Imperial,
then bounce on top of the huge red tiles
and bow — like a drunk — to the dancing whale,"
before I walk down to the yellow bus station
and buy my ticket at the frosted window
for Easton, Pennsylvania, or New York, New York.

ST. PATRICK'S DAY, 1979

I'm dreaming of the dahlias up there on the radiator,
starting to grow leaves,
and the jade plant getting a little fatter
and a little thicker every day.
I am the man with the rake, bent over with
emotional neck pains, standing in my yard getting
ready to be a garden adviser and a river prophet.

It's freezing — which is what peas like — and every
bird within half a mile is grating its beak
and foolishly chirping and coughing and whistling, half off key.
I have to make up my mind whether to look
back upstairs at the jade plant and the thick
white rag pulling it back in place or at the
sparkling river carrying everything — good and bad —
with it downhill to Trenton and Philadelphia,
fifty miles beyond my graveyard and my roaring spillway.

This spring song is for the drunks in New York,
and the Chinese witch hazel,
and the crow in New Jersey,
and the dying maple,
and the trellis and the rake and the shovel
and the small packet of new snap peas.

It is for the loud wind, and the clear shadows,
and the white cardboard and the red pen.
It is for the poet bent over his rows,
digging up huge chunks of dirt,
bowing and dancing like a white pigeon on Spring Street,
singing again about buried love and crazy renewal.

VISITING FLORIDA AGAIN

At Eleventh and Euclid I stood in front of an air
conditioner and listened to it whir. For just a second
I thought it was an insect screaming in anger
before it sucked up its enemy or ran into the hibiscus
to brood. For the first time
I gave thanks to my brother the machine,
my little friend, so out of place in the tropics,
so close now, compared to the hideous ichneumon
waving its long needle
or the velvet ant
searching for babies —
so misunderstood and abused.
— Shivering in the heat, I wanted to touch
some great yellow steam shovel or biplane,
something so oily and awkward
that it coughed and groaned for hours
before it moved its huge body
into position.
I felt as pure as Mayakovski
climbing into his aluminum vest,
as dear as Pico della Mirandola
watching his Jewish soul rise.
I joined the Shakers at their sweet stations,
the Anarchists

resting in the sun.
For just one second I was in London again
in the iron palace,
I was in Pittsburgh,
sitting in the old reference room,
reading Thomas Paine and William Blake and Peter Kropotkin,
creating my first dreams.

HANGING SCROLL

I have come back to Princeton three days in a row
to look at the brown sparrow in the apple branch.
That way I can get back in touch with the Chinese
after thirty years of silence and paranoid reproach.
It was painted seven hundred years ago by a Southerner
who was struggling to combine imitation and expression,
but nowhere is there a sense that calligraphy
has won the day, or anything lifeless or abstract.
I carry it around with me on a post card,
the bird in the center, the giant green leaves
surrounding the bird, the apples almost invisible,
their color and position chosen for obscurity —
somehow the sizes all out of whack, the leaves
too large, the bird too small, too rigid,
too enshrined for such a natural setting,
although this only comes slowly to mind
after many hours of concentration.

On my tree there are six starlings sitting and watching
with their heads in the air and their short tails under the twigs.
They are just faint shapes against a background of fog,
moving in and out of my small windows
as endless versions of the state of darkness.
The tree they are in is practically dead,

making it difficult for me to make plans
for my own seven hundred years
as far as critical position, or permanence.
— If the hanging scroll signifies a state
of balance, a state almost of tension
between a man and nature or a man and his dream,
then my starlings signify the tremendous
delicacy of life and the tenuousness of attachment.
This may sound too literary — too German —
but, for me, everything hangs in the balance
in the movement of those birds,
just as, in my painter,
his life may have been hanging from the invisible apple
or the stiff tail feathers or the minuscule feet.
I don't mean to say that my survival
depends upon the artistic rendering;
I mean that my one chance for happiness
depends on wind and strange loyalty and a little bark,
which I think about and watch and agonize over
day and night,
like a worried spirit
waiting for love.

A HUNDRED YEARS FROM NOW

A hundred years from now nobody will know who Zane Grey was
nor what the ten-cent pulp smelled like
nor what it was like to carry *Liberty* magazines on your back.
If you are bored to death by this then think of Wallace Stevens
when he first walked into the University of Pennsylvania library
and the memories he had of certain leather chairs,
or think of Ts'ai Yen in the land of frost and snow,
remembering his sweet mother.

I myself am searching for the purple sage that I can share
for all time with the poets of Akkadia and Sumeria.
I am starting with my river bottom, the twisted
sycamores and the big-leaved catalpas, making the connections
that will put Zane Grey in the right channel. I am
watching a very ancient Babylonian who looks something
like me or Allen Ginsberg before he shaved his beard off
pick up *The Border Legion* and *The Riders of the Trail*
from the dust. I am explaining him the spirit
of America behind our banality, our devotion
to the ugly and our suicidal urges;
how Zane Grey, once he saw the desert,
could not stop giving his life to it,
in spite of his dull imagination and stilted prose;
how the eternal is also here,

only the way to it is brutal.
O Babylonian, I am swimming in the deep off the island
of my own death and birth. Stay with me!

THE POEM OF LIBERATION

The smell of piss is what we have in the city
to remind us of the country and its dark ammonia.
In the subway it's like a patch of new lilac
or viburnum in the air or like that pocket
of cold water you swim in at Batsto
or that other pocket of water at Amagansett.
In the telephones it sinks in the metal plates
like the smell in a rug or a rotten sofa,
a stain you run away from in grief and anger.

Sometimes I walk in the East Side past the brownstones
on Fifty-second Street or the long sleek canopies
that almost cover the sidewalks from Fifth to Madison.
Then it's like remembering the stone walls in Italy
or the tiny alleys behind the bazaars in Africa.
Then I know, walking in front of Park East
or the Hampton House or the Penguin,
that New York will be the first city to go,
and we will no longer live like English,
hating the sight of sweet bananas and thick-armed
women smashing dice against the boards.

Across the street from St. John's there is a large
vegetable garden planted in the rubble

of a wrecked apartment house, as if to claim
the spirit back before it could be buried
in another investment of glass and cement.
There are thin maples and pieces of orange brick
and weeds and garbage as well as little rows
of beans and lettuce and hills of squash and melons.
It is a confused garden but I think the
soul of New York is there in the vague balance
of shape against shape and in the lush presence
of objects, from the blue cement fish pond
to the curved brick walk to the outdoor grille and chair;
a boxed-in mulch pit, iron candelabra, deep
irrigation ditches, delicate flower beds,
everything crowded into the smallest space.

I stand on the steps in front of the straining prophet,
looking across at the other two buildings, saved
by the squatters in 1970. I look at the splintered
doors and the pile of rubbish outside the windows
and make my own philosophical connections.
Behind the church, totally hidden from the street,
is another garden, planted by the women
of St. John's, this one a biblical
fantasy of trees and herbs and flowers,
from Matthew and John and Samuel, laid out in perfect
clusters, poplar from Genesis, reeds from Kings,
nettles from Job, lovely carob from Luke,
completely different from the other garden,
but not a mirror image of it
and not a sacred version of the profane,
one a vile parody of the other,
although these ideas flooded through my mind.

I fall asleep under the olive trees
thinking of Jezebel and Elijah.
I want to like one garden and hate the other

but I find myself loving both, both ideas,
both deeply thought out, both passionate.
I talk to the fat Englishman — the curator
of the church museum — about the two gardens
and the squatters and the church's benign role
and get his views on property, and mercy,
and study his tiny feet and row of books.
Finally I walk across the street again
to look at the People's Garden and plan my
little corner next to the climbing roses,
maybe a hosta or a bleeding heart.

My last hour is spent reading the poem
of liberation — in Spanish and English —
nailed up on the wire fence
and walking through the Plaza Caribe
under the slogans and the brown faces.
— At first I think it's hope again, hope played out
on a two-stringed instrument or a soggy drum,
Hebrew melancholy and Moorish wailing
under a fringed lamp, in a ruined chair,
but then I realize it's hope mixed in with memory
and not that other bitter stupid dream again,
stuck to the face like a drop of baby dew.
I love memory too, the weeping mouth
that will not let you go, the sweet smell drifting
through the alleys, the hum at the high window;
and I love the fact that, this time, no one will stand
with his straw hat in his hand in the marble courtroom
singing, "I love you, Kate Smith. I love you, I love you,
I love you, *presidente*, I love you, *señor* mayor."
I dig a hole in the ground
and pour in my mixture of meal and water.
I spread the roots out in three directions
and pack them in with dirt.
I leave by the southern gate

across the street from the Hungarian pastry
and walk down 111th like a Bedouin farmer,
like a Polish shepherd,
like a Korean rope master,
my small steel shovel
humming and singing in the blue dust.

ACACIA

In locust trees the roots run along the ground
and bury themselves in the sides of hills for survival.
They grow in roses and strawberries
and come from little sticks humbly and touchingly.
In three counties I am the only one who loves them;
I am the only one who reads about them in Ilick;
I am the only one who grieves when they turn brown and
die, or lie bent and broken in the rain.

Three summers ago I walked through the streets of Albi
with my friend Dave Burrows — who has since become Das Anudas —
and a French parasite and his little American wife.
We saw the locusts from the river not far from the brick
cathedral — made out of Protestant blood — not far from the huge
Toulouse-Lautrec collection housed in a palace,
something, it seemed to me then, like housing hundreds
of baby lambs or tons of fresh flowers
in the lobby or restaurant of a Howard Johnson's.

We argued for half an hour about the locust.
He told me it was now French but originally
it grew in southern China and India.
I told him it came from western Pennsylvania
and was brought to Europe in the nineteenth century.

He told me it was planted on the side of streets and in parks
because of its shade and its ornamental qualities.
I told him it was practically a weed in America,
that farmers valued it mainly for fence posts.

I remember his wife — she was displaced;
her eyes were round, her skin almost transparent.
We ate a late supper in the square near the railroad
station and her voice had already assumed that
flat ungoverned tone I have heard in dozens
of museums and restaurants from London to Heraklion.
When she and I talked English her vile husband
frowned and barked at her in his southern French,
and when I shook hands with her to say good-by
and kissed her on the side of her small mouth
it was like stripping those tiny leaves from their stems
or smelling again the sweetest of all blossoms,
like being again in the Allegheny mountains
where locusts first started, four million years ago.

And that, my love, is a continent and a half away
from Albi, where the northern French descended
on the southern French and in the name of Jesus
destroyed their culture and their strange religion
and made them build a tributary cathedral
where Das Anudas and I walked all morning,
noting every detail of the pink fortress,
fainting from the beauty,
growing hungry from the climb,
changed forever halfway through our lives.

YOUR ANIMAL

The final end of all but purified souls
is to be swallowed up by Leviathan,
or to be bound with fiery chains and flogged
with 70 stripes of fire.
I walk along the mule path dreaming of my weaknesses
and praying to the ducks for forgiveness.
Oh there is so much shit in the universe
and my walks, like yours,
are more and more slippery and dangerous.
I love a duck for being almost like a vegetable.
I love him because his whole body can be consumed,
because there is no distance between him and his watery offal.
Your animal is almost human,
distant from his waste,
struggling to overcome the hated matter,
looking up with horrified white eyes,
eternally hunting for space in the little islands of Riverside Drive
and the fenced-in parks of the Village.

I love duck and potatoes, duck and red beets,
duck and orange juice.
I love the head of duck dipped in sugar,
I love chocolate duck with chipolota sausages,
fragrant crisp duck mixed with shrimp and pork.

I love the webs and the heart; I love the eggs
preserved in lime and potash, completely boned duck
filled with ham and chestnuts, fried duck with pineapple
and canned red cherries or sections of tangerine.

This is a poem against gnosticism;
it is a poem against the hatred of the flesh
and all the vicious twists and turns we take
to calm our frightened souls.
It is a poem celebrating the eating of duck
and all that goes with it.
It is a poem I am able to write after walking every day
through the flocks, and loving the babies, and watching them slip
down the mud sides and float into the current.
It is a poem about shooting galleries and cardboard heads,
about hunters and their checkered hats and frozen fingers,
about snow-white cloths and steaming laced-up birds
and waiters standing in little regiments
getting ready to run in among the tables and start carving.
— It is my poem against the starving heart.
It is my victory over meanness.

THE ROSE WAREHOUSE

Ah tunnel cows,
watching over my goings out
and my comings in,
you preside, like me, over your own butchery.

I always look for you
when I go back to Pennsylvania,
driving under the rusty piers
and up Fortieth Street.

All of New York must be laid out for you up there,
the slope on Park Avenue,
the moon on the river,
the roof of the Port Authority.

I feel like putting up my own head,
the head of Gerald Stern,
on the side of the Rose Warehouse, his glasses slipping off,
his tears falling one by one on Eleventh Avenue.

I want to see if he will sing
or if he will stare out at the blue sky forever and forever.
I want to see if he's a god
and feels like murmuring a little in the lost tongue

or if he's one of those black humans,
still mourning after thirty years —
some German Jew
talking about Berlin,

the town that had everything;
some man of love
who dug his own grave and entered there;
some sorrowful husband

refusing to wash, refusing to listen to music,
cutting his flesh, rubbing dust in his hair,
throwing in dirt, throwing in flowers,
kissing the shovel good-by, kissing the small shovel.

THE RED COAL

Sometimes I sit in my blue chair trying to remember
what it was like in the spring of 1950
before the burning coal entered my life.

I study my red hand under the faucet, the left one
below the grease line consisting of four feminine angels
and one crooked broken masculine one

and the right one lying on top of the white porcelain
with skin wrinkled up like a chicken's
beside the razor and the silver tap.

I didn't live in Paris for nothing and walk
with Jack Gilbert down the wide sidewalks
thinking of Hart Crane and Apollinaire

and I didn't save the picture of the two of us
moving through a crowd of stiff Frenchmen
and put it beside the one of Pound and Williams

unless I wanted to see what coals had done
to their lives too. I say it with vast affection,
wanting desperately to know what the two of them

talked about when they lived in Pennsylvania
and what they talked about at St. Elizabeth's
fifty years later, looking into the sun,

40,000 wrinkles between them,
the suffering finally taking over their lives.
I think of Gilbert all the time now, what

we said on our long walks in Pittsburgh, how
lucky we were to live in New York, how strange
his great fame was and my obscurity,

how we now carry the future with us, knowing
every small vein and every elaboration.
The coal has taken over, the red coal

is burning between us and we are at its mercy —
as if a power is finally dominating
the two of us; as if we're huddled up

watching the black smoke and the ashes;
as if knowledge is what we needed and now
we have that knowledge. Now we have that knowledge.

The tears are different — though I hate to speak
for him — the tears are what we bring back to the
darkness, what we are left with after our

own escape, what, all along, the red coal had
in store for us as we moved softly,
either whistling or singing, either listening or reasoning,

on the gray sidewalks and the green ocean;
in the cars and the kitchens and the bookstores;
in the crowded restaurants, in the empty woods and libraries.

THERE IS WIND, THERE ARE MATCHES

A thousand times I have sat in restaurant windows,
through mopping after mopping, letting the ammonia clear
my brain and the music from the kitchens
ruin my heart. I have sat there hiding
my feelings from my neighbors, blowing smoke
carefully into the ceiling, or after I gave
that up, smiling over my empty plate
like a tired wolf. Today I am sitting again
at the long marble table at Horn and Hardart's,
drinking my coffee and eating my burnt scrapple.
This is the last place left and everyone here
knows it; if the lights were turned down, if the
heat were turned off, if the banging of dishes stopped,
we would all go on, at least for a while, but then
we would drift off one by one toward Locust or Pine.
— I feel this place is like a birch forest
about to go; there is wind, there are matches, there is snow,
and it has been dark and dry for hundreds of years.
I look at the chandelier waving in the glass
and the sticky sugar and the wet spoon.
I take my handkerchief out for the sake of the seven
years we spent in Philadelphia and the
steps we sat on and the tiny patches of lawn.
I believe now more than I ever did before

in my first poems and more and more I feel
that nothing was wasted, that the freezing nights
were not a waste, that the long dull walks and
the boredom, and the secret pity, were
not a waste. I leave the paper sitting,
front page up, beside the cold coffee,
on top of the sugar, on top of the wet spoon,
on top of the grease. I was born for one thing,
and I can leave this place without bitterness
and start my walk down Broad Street past the churches
and the tiny parking lots and the thrift stores.
There was enough justice, and there was enough wisdom,
although it would take the rest of my life — the next
two hundred years — to understand and explain it;
and there was enough time and there was enough affection
even if I did tear my tongue
begging the world for one more empty room
and one more window with clean glass
to let the light in on my last frenzy.
— I do the crow walking clumsily over his meat,
I do the child sitting for his dessert,
I do the poet asleep at his table,
waiting for the sun to light up his forehead.
I suddenly remember every ruined life,
every betrayal, every desolation,
as I walk past Tasker toward the city of Baltimore,
banging my pencil on the iron fences,
whistling Bach and Muczynski through the closed blinds.

THE-WAY-WE-WERE LOUNGE

This is the kind of place I loved when I walked
across Italy looking every night for open
spaces. I would have lain on my back
staring up at the two rusty cedar trees
and the broken notes and the tilted cocktail glass.
I would have sung myself to sleep
thinking about Padua and little Verona with the rose walls.
I was like a gorilla, making a new
bed every night, digging a hole so I could
lie on the ground without breaking my bones.
I was a believer — the one time in my life —
traveling from town to town with my marble notebook
full of dark signs and incantations.
I would have loved the swaying pole
and the white sidewalk.
I would have waited for hours
to put my shoes on
and wash my face at the iron spigot.
I would have stood up like a devout shadow
to look at the moon again in the first daylight.

WAVING GOOD-BY

I wanted to know what it was like before we
had voices and before we had bare fingers and before we
had minds to move us through our actions
and tears to help us over our feelings,
so I drove my daughter through the snow to meet her friend
and filled her car with suitcases and hugged her
as an animal would, pressing my forehead against her,
walking in circles, moaning, touching her cheek,
and turned my head after them as an animal would,
watching helplessly as they drove over the ruts,
her smiling face and her small hand just visible
over the giant pillows and coat hangers
as they made their turn into the empty highway.

IN THESE SHADOWS

All that I know about the rose
and the paper snowflake and the living goddess
is in these shadows — the rose's limpness,
the snowflake's fluorescence, the goddess's violent
anger. All that I ever learned
is suddenly altered
and all the cunning and pain is reduced
to a dark image where the body falls.

Oh sweetness, sweetness! I can walk the length
of my dying maple; I can live again
in its old arms; I can watch it reach
out to the river, or stand like the first man
for hours in the cold sun,
looking at the soft ice,
sliding over the leaves,
disappearing in the blue water.

DEAR MOLE

Dear mole, I have forgotten you!
Living under the dahlias, making highways
under the pines, coming up to sniff
blindly, like John Ruskin,
at the pink chrysanthemums and the red berries
hanging from the ruined viburnum.

Everything depends on your sponginess,
the world you created with your
shoulders and claws,
the long tunnels and the quiet rooms
where you can wander — like Ruskin —
dreaming of smooth floors and vaulted ceilings.

He was like you,
always cramming and ramming, spluttering in disgust,
hating repression, living apart from others,
adoring mountains, drifting with the vortices,
hemorrhaging a little,
loving high sounds, loving the crystal orders.

He was like you,
following the laws of the fourteenth century,
envious of the fish,

curiously breathless and obsesssed with shadows,
loving small girls, living deep in Hell,
always beginning, always starting over,
his head down, his poor soul warbling and wailing.

MY HAND

I have put my hand in a baby shepherd's mouth
and watched him whine with pleasure.
I have seen him roll on his back
with his white stomach facing the sun
and paw helplessly.
I think he is full of some low form of love,
something that Dante would have pitied
as he moved from heaven to heaven,
something akin to the drowned buttercup
or the red woodpecker swinging on his bag of fat.
There would be a crease at the corner of Dante's eye,
a roundness in his cheek,
that is for that animal alone —
a tiny sign
interrupting his climbing and his falling,
his concentration on justice and liberation.

THESE BIRDS

These birds burst in and out of their shadows
as if they alone in all the world were breathing,
as if their violent heartbeats were the only hope,
as if the snow could withstand two more contradictions,
as if they could defy the life of all sanity.

They bring their bodies with them
and walk into the wires and through the trees
as if they could drink and eat with impunity,
as if their wings gave them the right to stand there,
as if there were not another life to think of,
as if one stillness were not overlying the other,
as if they had not already created the first darkness,
as if dreaming and not dreaming were the same,
as if the sky could save them,
as if they could depend again on their own savagery.

ARTHUR'S LILY

I could never feel sorry for Arthur Vogelsang,
resting among his kafir-lilies and his phoenix tree.
I could never say there he is
in Los Angeles wiping his eyes from the smog
and leaping across the great crack in his sidewalk.
He has a whole desert to live in without poets;
he has the letter of Ezra Pound cursing jellyfish;
he has the city of Baltimore to remember.
— I could never drop a tear for him,
knowing he is standing by his crooked mailbox;
I could never lure him with our warm water
or touch him with our snow,
knowing he is buying a white Chrysler,
knowing he is throwing the grapefruit;
I could never drag him back,
knowing he is talking to the cement frog,
knowing he is practicing footprints,
knowing he is planning another ecstatic voyage.

THE PICASSO POEM

It was when the bridal wreaths were all out
and those smelly weeds, the graduation speakers,
were blooming on one green lawn after another
that I sat on my porch trying to make up my mind
about the Pablo Picasso I loved the most.
It was Sunday morning and the *New York Times*
was full of his glory; it was Sunday
and the skinny runners were out
and the iris were combing their tiny beards
and the lilacs were waving a dark good-by.
I wanted to drive a 1936 Pontiac
to New York City to see the exhibition.
I wanted to drive through sweet New Jersey with the picnic
basket bumping my knee and the line of trees
keeping the sun out from Phillipsburg to Newark.
Over and over again I thought of him
in the 1930's and I thought of the paintings
he did and I thought of the France he loved,
all plump and modern and corrupt.
He was 55 in 1936 and slipping
through the silence before his next flowering;
he was moving from one hard place to another,
dipping his hand and smearing the white canvas.

— I think I'd have to choose between the woman
with a hat or the one with rope for a face
or the one reclining — with stars — or the one in a nightmare
ripping apart a handkerchief;
or maybe the goat; or maybe the bicycle handle.
  On June ninth I stood peacefully in line
waiting to crawl through the numbered rooms.
I was so quiet little birds were resting
on my soft shoulder and little leaves were growing
from my legs and arms.
Somewhere, inside my chest, a heart was pounding,
and I was listening again, a little thinner
and a little whiter than the last time.
I walked through the birches, I walked through the dry rain,
I bent down and ran my fingers
through the black dirt. Three hours from then
I would walk down that line from the other side,
dreaming — I think — of my own next darkness.
God save Fifth Avenue, God save New York
from my assault. God let me drive
across the Pulaski Skyway singing those great
songs; leaning out the little window
and staring down at the Jersey swamp;
smelling that sulphur; driving up into the sun
and looking back on those iron lamps; looking forward
over and over to the future, streets in the sky,
towers in the ground, dancing people, little
dogs for every family. I waver between
that world and this. I travel back and forth
between the two. I lose myself
and crawl off singing or come back crying,
my face wet with misery, my eyes deep holes
where the dream was lost, my hands up in their favorite
position, the two unbroken fingers
cutting the air,

thirty feet above the river,
beside the hostas and the mugho pine,
the dirty bottles and the stones
fixing the boundary for another summer.

THE ROAR

That was the last time I would walk up those five
flights with a woman in tow, standing
in the hall patiently trying my keys,
listening to my heart pounding from the climb.

And the last time I would sit in front of the
refrigerator, drinking white wine and asking
questions, and lecturing — like a spider —
and rubbing my hand through my hair — like a priest.

Look at me touch the burning candle
with my bare palm and press a rusty knife
against my left eyelid while she undresses.

Look at me rise through the cool airshaft
and snore at the foot of the bed with one hand
on her knee and one hand touching the white floor,

the red and blue beacon of Empire
just beyond those little houses
as familiar now as my crippled birch

and the endless roar out there
as sweet as my own roar
in my other dream, on the cold and empty river.

FOR NIGHT TO COME

I am giving instructions to my monkey
on how to plant a pine tree. I am telling
him to water the ground for hours before
he starts to dig and I am showing him
how to twist the roots so the limbs will bend
in the right direction.
                        He is weeping
because of the sweet air, and remembering
our canoe trip, and how we went swimming
on Mother's Day. And I am remembering
the holiness and how we stopped talking
after we left Route 30. I show him the tree
with the two forks and the one with the
stubs and the one with the orange moss
underneath, and we make our nest in a clearing
where the wind makes hissing noises and the sun
goes through our heavy clothes.
                                All morning we lie
on our backs, holding hands, listening to birds,
and making little ant hills in the sand.
He shakes a little, maybe from the cold,
maybe a little from memory,
maybe from dread. I think we are lost,
only a hundred yards from the highway,

and we will have to walk around in fear,
or separate and look for signs before
we find it again.
                    We pick a small green tree,
thick with needles and cones and dangling roots,
and put it in the trunk on top of the blanket,
and straighten the branches out, and smooth the hairs.
All the way back we will be teary and helpless,
loving each other in the late afternoon,
and only when we have made the first cut
and done the dance
and poured in the two bushels of humus
and the four buckets of water
and mixed it in with dirt and tramped it all down
and arranged and rearranged the branches
will we lie back and listen to the chimes
and stop our shaking
and close our eyes a little
and wait for night to come
so we can watch the stars together,
like the good souls we are,
a hairy man and a beast
hugging each other in the white grass.

HERE I AM WALKING

Here I am walking between Ocean and Neptune,
sinking my feet in mile after mile of wet life.
I am practically invisible
in the face of all this clutter,
either straying near the benches over the buried T-shirts
or downhill in the graveyard
where the burned families are sleeping in the sun
or eating dry lunch among the corpses.
I will finish walking in two hours
and eat my sandwich in the little park
beside the iron Methodist.
This is the first step.
Tomorrow I will start again in Barnegat
and make my way toward Holgate or Ventnor.
This is something different
than it was even five years ago.
I have a second past to rake over
and search through — another 2000 miles of seashore
to account for.
— I am still making my mind up
between one of those art deco hotels
in Miami Beach, a little back room on a court
where you could almost be in Cuba or
Costa Rica of the sweet flesh, and

a wooden shack in one of the mosquito marshes
in Manahawkin or the Outer Banks.
I am planning my cup of tea
and my sweet biscuit,
or my macaroni soup
and my can of sardines.
If I spent the morning washing shirts
I would read for two hours
before I slept through the afternoon.
If I walked first, or swam,
I might feel like writing down words
before I went in for coffee, or more hot water.
I will sit on the black rocks
to make my connections,
near the small basin of foam.
I will look at the footprints
going in and out of the water
and dream up a small blue god to talk to.
I will be just where I was
twenty-five years ago,
breathing in salt,
snorting like a prophet,
turning over the charred wood;
just where I was then,
getting rid of baggage,
living in dreams,
finding a way to change, or sweeten, my clumsy life.